# Rebuilding
# SCABS

# Rebuilding SCABS

## Part II of the "Scabs" Series

poetry by
### L.Q. Murphy

L.Q. MURPHY ◆ FRESNO, CA

# Copyright Page

# Dedication

\-   For YOU...

# Table of Contents

# Acknowledgments

There are too many to thank, but I would like to thank my friends and family first if I began someplace. They have sacrificed so I can be myself every day.

I am inspired by the people who came from nothing and earned their way to the dominant class of society. By nothing, I mean people who were shoved to the side, doubted, laughed at, bullied, lied to, discriminated against, and judged unfairly-negative by the mass of society. The people I respect are the ones that found a way to climb to the top echelons of society. Here is a list of people who did not let their dire environments hold them to a lower standard of living: Denzel Washington, Oprah Winfrey, Robert L. Johnson, Nipsey Hustle, Malcolm X, J.K. Rowling, Colin Powell, Mike Tyson, Steve Harvey, Floyd Mayweather Jr., Judge Joe Brown, Robert T. Kiyosaki, and Napoleon Hill. They left clues to follow for success. Clues that help to improve their living conditions.

This is what I can relate to. I can respect the people who want to help every person who desires to improve their life. Real-world heroes consider the lives from the lowest classism to the lives in the highest stratosphere of classism. These are the people I tend to acknowledge the most.

And I can not forget to thank the universe and that highest power in the universe that continues to let me live and breathe another day. Thank you.

# Introduction

This book aims to remedy the scabs that strike the hearts of many people.

I, the author, used the writings in this book as a form of therapy. Sorrow, regret, bad experiences, strange experiences, sad outcomes, and dysfunctional lifestyle habits fractured my soul. So, I wrote to find solace.

From the advice and persuasion of others, I made these private writings available to you. You will find solace knowing you do not walk those desolate roads alone—those unforgiving jagged, bumpy roads that cut the flesh we use to laugh and smile.

Suppose you, the reader, will allow me to frame this book. In that case, you will immediately realize that the poems listed are not in order of significance. Just as in life, the poetry written in this book is in random order. The poetry I write is abstract and deep in thinking. From my observation, life is abstract. It is in that abstraction that life found meaning.

We are all different, and that can not be more evident than in the imagination we dwell. That is nothing profound but what is deep is our ability to create physically that which first appeared mentally. This collection of poetry is what emerged for me, and now it is your exclusive visual on the scabs that I still attempt to rebuild. Enjoy!

The

# FIRST

and

# ONLY

Chapter

# Fall Scab... Fall

When a scab has fallen
      Below
           Below
                Below leaves
                Beneath the dust
                Beyond the wind...

When a scab has fallen
Is the grief over?
Is the sky clear?
Is the end of healing near?

                            It is like this
                            When a scab has
                    fallen.

# Days More Sunny

No days
No days
No more sunny
Than watching the goose.

Fly by.
Waddle by.

What?

Are you proud.
Shoulders back.
Dividing crowds.

The goose had entered.
That goose got hooked.
That goose was another
Goose
That got cooked.

# Partake

No More watching scabs crack
The time has arrived

Where ponds have dead cats
And the waves
Have eyes

Split scabs
Flapping scabs
Of flapping scabs
Many
Many
Disgusting flapping scabs

In the sight
Of many souls
Scabs break
Scabs take
Scabs heal
A life of scabs
To partake

# Cut Grass in the Park

Now walk
Around the park
Where the legs cross
And cross more

The scent of gas
The waft of chopped grass
I move right past

For in a day
Like the spin of the earth
I stay the course
Through this life
To my grave

# You ever heard of that guy?

You ever heard of that guy?
One step behind
Is it me

He tears flesh apart
Inside
His insides

He punished his dreams
Beat them down
With a rock

He sealed happy thoughts
With burning lava
And sharp rocks

You ever heard of that guy
It's the brain in this guy
He's insane... this guy

You ever heard of that guy?

Hey You!
You ever heard of that guy?

# Four Cups

Four cups
One blood
One water
One milk
One mud

Could you imagine
The one cup
I consumed?

NO... I bet not.

I consumed them all.
But Why?
Why? Why? Why?

I could tell you why
But you wouldn't get it

I could spread a lie
But you wouldn't see it

Four cups
One blood
One water
One milk
One mud

Don't let your life
Become a dud

# The Point

The point
Yes. That point
Don't point
Poke and pierce
But don't point
What's the point?
You don't see.
Maybe you can't see.
Should I point
I know what I said.
But you seem blind.
Like the point has evaded you.
I've been tagged.
Can you see my pain?
My blood.
Someone once said, "That's the point of the point."
A bullet?
Blunter than point.
More like cruel than to the point.
Just let me make my point.
My rule. The point. I break now.
Now I point.
Up. There. Yes. There.
The head. The point.
Follow that point. That direction.
Sound like the harp.
Stay from beneath the tarp.
Listen to your heart.
The harp of your heart.
That's the point.
Don't be cruel. Follow the rule and remember the point.
Follow the point. That's the point. Do you see the point?

# Cat or Rat

I heard a rat
Yup! I said that.
Over there.
Look again
Listen again
See it. The rat.
Near the cat.
It squeaks. It peeps.
You can't hear huh?
Your ears forward... huh?
Behind you. Behind your back.
A rat. That rat.
Who said that?
The fat cat?
The cat posted up with the black hat?
The cat?
That cat is really a rat.
A fat rat.
More like a bat that lurks at night
In the dark. Hissing blood.
The rats of rats.
Speaking.
Talking when they should be walking.
Disguised by obscurity.
Who said "who said"?
Ears stretched wide.
Legitimate cat.
More like a certified rat.
Behind your back.
Yup.
That's a rat.
Yup!
It's a rap.

# Where is My Stick

Hand me that stick.
I have a tick.
It sucks my blood.
My genetics.
My future. My past.
All of me.
Many of me.

I need that stick.
I have an itch.
It hurts.
It bites.
This prick.
I can't reach without a stick.
How does my future taste?
How about my past?
Is it strong?
Will it last?

Ouch. Ouch.
Your chomp and chew sting.
You devour my future with just a single sting.
You've made your mark.
Your back to me.
Deep in the dark.
No.
I think I need a bigger stick.

Sucked dry by a tick.
My past.
The future of things to pass.
I'm out of blood you tick.
You make me sick.
And all because
I did not carry a big stick.

# All Red

Nails cut.
Still slicing.
Still dicing.

Salt and pepper.
I shake it up.
Bless You.
Now shush-up.

On your knees.
Don't look now.
You're dead.

In a silk sheet.
In a bed.
All red. All red.

All I've read...
From the wise.
From the dead.

No bed. No rest.
Just the best.
Test to test.

# Tell You

You know that
Scuffy told Scratchy
And then
Scratchy told Fancy
And then
Fancy told Billy
And then
Billy told Philly
And then
Philly told Pusher
And then
Pusher told Holder
And then
Holder told Bolder
And then
Bolder told Colder
And then
Colder told Summer
And then
Summer told Fall
And then
Fall told Winter
And then
Winter told Spring
And then
Spring told Mother
And then
Mother told Father
And then
Father told Seed
And then
Seed told Earth
"I forgot."
"I forgot."
"Oh no, I forgot what to tell you."

# You May See What I See

Lift up that leaf
What do you see?
Is it you or is it me?

Detective. Figure this out.
What do you see?
A crawler. A slug.
In the shade of this tree.

In the chest. The slug.
The plug. Tugged. I saw.
Slimy. Nasty slug. It crawled.

Slug one. Slug two. Slugs decay.
Brush the leaves away.

Savage.
Harsh.
It's only March.

What a place to be.
Beneath the leaves.

Slugs.
Leaves.
You.
Me.
Slugs always leave a trail.
Where they are found.
Read a tale.

The circle of life.
That's all that's left.
The plug disconnected.
It's all Perceptive.

# The White Doves took Flight

That night
The white doves took flight...
The night types.
No.
Just a life of fright.

Brush fires burning orange
Red flames. Blue flames.
Across the range.
No Moonlight.
Trees. Leaves.
Naked and terrified.

Stretching upward.
Attempting to evade the heat.
The shape-shifter approaches.
A silhouette against the glow.
Reaching towards the heaven.
To live ever more.
A simple plea.
What's the fee?

The breeze blows to and fro.
Swift.
A dance for two.
A dance of peace.
The dance of war.
It was like that on that night the doves took flight.
A dance of sacrifice.
They say that the wind and fire asked the tree to dance.
Strangers in the night.
Till death do them part.
It was like that.
White doves
Threading the dark.

# <u>Where Is the Love</u>

Help me down
Don't make a sound
Step by step
Pound by pound

Down we go
Quiet and slow
Hill by hill
Don't slow our roll

Look below
It's loud
It's crowded
Where's your love?
It's been shrouded

Basement floor
Down
More and more
Shallow and void
Just show me the door.

# Flying Black Rat

It squeaks
It reeks
And it peeks

It's high
It's shy
In the sky

A bat
Just sat
Atop my hat
And now I must not cry!

# Take Your Pick

Help me quick
Take your pick
Back or forth
It's your pick

Shoulders burn
It's your turn
Icebergs ahead
My scabs are dead

Left foot. Right foot.
What's next? Which foot?

Reaching for roses
As my scab closes

Hair thin emotions
Might like oceans
Egg on a knife edge
Watch the devil's ledge

Fly downside up
Hand glued to cup
No kind of mind
This light of mine

Help me quick
Take your pick

# The Deadly Daze

Death days approached.
The deadly daze
Encroached.

The tree with thick bark.
Legs bending wrong.
No socks.
Black Pit-Bull clench.
No bark.

Drift from the python's grip
Let your breath go.
Time's hold is neutral
Like escrow.

Don't trip.
A bog. A log.
Lost in the fog.
Mush, mush
In life's smelly fog.

The fog only gets thicker
Your mind
Tries to keep up
With your heart's ticker.

Death unfolds. Shapeless. Bold.
Hits quick like smoke.
Sit down.
Check-in.
It's cold.

# Tell a Chicken

Tell a chicken to fly.
Tell the richest to help.
Let the arrogant cry.
Make the wolverine yelp.

# A Cave Too Deep

I need your help.
I am all alone.
A cave too deep
To see the light.

Bare.
I hold the weight of
Bats and birds.

The passerby stares.
Others?
Nasty glares.

Too old to move?
Have I lost my groove?

Who is it that wants me?
A slithery spirit.
More like an ocean wave.

My cave is empty.
A dusty cave.
I regret
That all I did
Was behave.

Who passes my sleepless cry?
The clawing winds?
The ghosts of friends?

I'm all alone.
No chance.
No hope.
I need your help...
Before the clock's brutal choke.

# The Growling Scene

The neighborhood was quiet
I closed the door behind me
What's this? The hallway was lathered.
Broken frames. Fallen shelves. Candles scattered.

My heart-beat thundered.
Maybe dark syrup this far from the table.

Chest cavity don't fail me now.
Just expand and compress.
And don't forget to wet the throat.
I see... I see... I see... A person. A dog.

This is my home, but who were they.
Growling. The canine teeth glowing.
But... The person.
Who... and do I smell iron?

Suddenly, a shape moved.
I snapped my sight.
A sickle. It hit. Torso. No pain. Just cold.
Split and splat.
Swift swipes.
My guts side by side with gravity.

I'm on my knee. I can't see mercy.
Just a silhouette.
Too tall to organize.
Still, my hand is out for mercy.

A token lands in my palm.
The toll will be paid.
My soul is finished. It fades away,
Away.

# My Pearl

I pushed the pearl
Off the table.

And
Off the table
I heard
A ting,
A plink,
A clink
And a crack.

Whoops.
Never again.
Will I
Allow
My
Precious pearl
To fall
And hit the ground.

# Ice cream sat on a porch

I rocked back and forth
A summer breeze
Wind fluttered the tips of the grassland
I sat my ice cream nearby
The wind although invisible
Had my eye.
I wondered
Could that be I.
To move the world and fly
To dance with every leaf
To flirt with every blade of grass.
To be free and dance and prance.
I was no longer sitting.
I began running
With the wind.
Along its side.
Exuberance I could not hide.
The time had come and it had gone.
And when I came back to my chair. I sat.
No Ice. Just cream on a porch.
Just my dream on this porch.

# That's the line

Hop, hop, hop.
That's it. That's the line.
Go left. Go left again.
That's it. That's the line.

Wait. Don't move.
That's it. That's the line.
Look what the bird landed on.
That's it. That's the line.

Move on your toes. You tripped.
That's it. That's the line.
Swim far. Oh no.
That's it. That's the line.

You're lost. You wanna go home.
That's it. That's the line.
Buy you fun. Buy you sun.
That's it. That's the line.

You need gold. Dig here. Dig there.
That's it. That's the line.
Electricity. You need a zap?
That's it. That's the line.

You're spinning. You want brakes.
That's it. That's the line.
Your life, it's sinking.
That's it. That's the line.

I see your heart is cracked Love.
That's it. That's the line.
The god you say. Prayer.
That's it. That's the line.

The easy life.
Just never cross that there.
That's it. That's the line.
The line thinner than baby hair.

# The Compass Bird

One wing red
One wing blue
The bird looked purple
Each time it flew.

The first kid said
The bird was red
The second kid said
The bird was blue

Daddy
Said
The bird
Was red and blue

Mommy
Said
The Bird
Was purple

The dog
Just barked.
The cat
Just slept.

The bird flew back around
Landed on a nearby tree branch
The bird side-eyed them all
And said,

When I fly east I am blue
When I fly west I am red
When I fly north or south
I am purple at best.

# I Have a Mark

I have a mark
It's a mark I say
I can see it
I can see it all day

I have a mark I tell you
It won't go away
I scrub in a tub
I scrub all day

I have a mark right there
I scratch it with my nails
My nails won't grow back
My nails won't grow in a day

I have a mark I was told
It was moldy. It was gross.
It keeps growing and growing
It keeps growing all day

I have a mark inside my head
It's everywhere I go
It burrows holes in my mind
It burrows holes all day

# I Need a Hand

I got some thing
I got something to say
Should I tell you?
Will you be afraid?

I knew a kid
He was a boy
And all he wanted
Was a toy

This boy you see
He was me
I needed love
That I could see

I was ten
When it all began
A tiny pain
Within my hand

At age eleven
That hand was gone
No love to save me
Just a hug from mom

An old man once told me
"In life you must give a hand
And you will get one back."
So, I wait for my loving hand.

# I Have a Sweet Tooth

I need money
For some sweet honey
I have a sweet tooth

Cupcakes with sprinkles
And a milkshake that twinkles
I have a sweet tooth

Cherry pies baked fresh
Cotton candy the best
I have a sweet tooth

Colorful gumballs roll down
Sour gummi worms abound
I have a sweet tooth

Chocolate chip cookies stacked high
Fruity gummy bears fall from the sky
I have a sweet tooth

My sweet tooth
It hurts
It's starving
Needs sugar

My sweet tooth
It's mad
It's swelling
Who is it fooling?

# Heard What I Said?

Help me cross
The riverbed
Help me cross
Heard what I said?

I can use some stilts
Or a tall unicycle
To help me cross
This deep riverbed

The riverbed
Holds catfish bones
Where is the water?
It's dry as bones

Help me cross
My stilts went crack
The cycle went crunch
I'm stuck in time
My destiny has a hunch

My heel bones are dead
How much blood had to shed?
Have you heard what I said?
What has died in this river bed?

# 15 - Fifteen

Fifteen years ago
I was there
The same
No fame

Fifteen months ago
I felt the same
Always present
Not understood

Fifteen weeks ago
Like years ago
Like tears ago
Here we go

Fifteen days ago
Felt as yesterday
Felt as useless
Felt it go

Fifteen hours ago
I could not escape myself
I know something has changed
But what is it?

Fifteen minutes ago
I ate my last meal. I assure.
Graham crackers and peanut butter
The best. A childhood favorite.

Fifteen seconds ago
Fifteen seconds ago

# I Made These Walls

I made my walls
Boulder by boulder
Angry and tall
Shoulder to shoulder

Red skin stains
Scabs stuck to my shoulders
Smell the iron
Coming from the wall of boulders

Measured thoughts are the formula
A measure dangerous for some
If your recipe fails
Reformulate the thoughts that come

Scabs unstable
Cruel to some
A lab that alters
The life to come

My life be altered
By a father gone
Alone in these walls
The life for some

# It Will End

She
The lady in the yellow skirt

Has
The old man's heart

Seen
By many. A cruel way to make a living.

Her
Deception unfolded by those who care.

End
It now they say. Now she begs. Click-clack-boom.

# My First Thought Is

My first thought is about my first thought
Did I know I was thinking?
Was the moment odd? Was the moment even?

My first thought of apples.
Are they good for you?
Why are they red?

My first thought of God.
Is it she who made you?
Does she prefer us dead?

My first thought of Mom.
Was I made inside of you?
Is wisdom what you said?

My first thought of you.
Hurting others is what you do?
Is your chisel worth my dread?

My first thought of I.
What can this mind and body do?
Will there be order in my head?

My first thought should have been my last thought.
For thought has brought
The sorrows of my day and the sorrows of my ways.
The swinging arm of my clock is all I've been taught.

# A Hill of Scabs

I said kick upward
Dice and sway your head.
Slice the air
That's it. Bow your head.

Rolling down.
Spinning fast.
A hill of scabs
With bloody rags.

I yelled to you
Life isn't fair.
You sprayed tears
That sliced the air.

I consulted my books
I flipped over stones
I shouted the questions
I even whispered to bones

Bounce to skip
Skip to bounce
Your head rolls
As your final sight goes.

# The Glimmering Stone

The glimmering stone
In my eye made home
Setting up shop
A picture. A tone.

The glimmering stone
It built on its home
The back of my mind.
Carved windows to brighten its home.

The glimmering stone
It burrowed this time
Down in my chest
Flipped a light switch. Shinning its best.

The glimmering stone
It burrowed deeper
Down deep in my gut
The glimmer rooted itself

The glimmering stone
Now in my pocket
You built your home
Using my two hands

The glimmering stone
The more intelligent than all
In history and books
You still stand tall

# Scabs That Fold

Scabs that fold
Why be black
Why be red
Why looks so old?

The scab that folds
Splintered pains
Bad fashion
Sickened bulge

The scab that bleeds
Why by my feet?
Why past my seat?
What do you need?

The blood that's cold
When do you leak?
Where do you seek?
When do you fold?

The blood that rolls
Past my lips
Past my heart
And, Past my lips
Look it there.
Too cold to move.
Too old to dribble
Too sad to move.
Scabs be formed.
It will be worn
Scabs a plenty
My scabs are torn.

# **The Offset View**

This view has been
Offset
By you

The straight and narrow
Offset
By two

My mind is blind
Offset
By he

My corral of sins
Offset
By she

My ears bent downward
Offset
By feet

My death in simple terms
Offset
By heat

My universe
Offset
By none

My offset view
Offset
By time

# Think Not Good... Not Straight

I cannot think
Not good
Not straight
Not great

Why can I not think?
I have a brain
I can walk
I can talk

I just cannot think
I ate my apple
I jogged a mile
Orange-Juice I drank

My thoughts are stuck I think
Behind the sink
Behind that car
Behind my back. I think.

I think I just hate when I think
I think my stomach bowels groan
I think my eyeballs roll
I think a thought makes my body turn cold

My thoughts will come when I'm old I think
I snore on a death bred I think.
This be my end I think.
My last thought has come and gone I think.

# Flip the Dictionary

Flip, flip, flip
Flip the dictionary
A red canary
What do you wanna bury?

It's scary. Have you seen me go to work?
I grip, grab... it's scary. It's my little perk.

And what I do with liars
I save them for my pliers.
No. Not the tires.
A vroooooommmm to your tooommmmmb.
Smell the brains. They're yours.
They're being pulled from your nose.

From your ear... do you hear?
It's your mind... and it's mine.
Just doing time in your mind.
Pay attention. I got your spine.

It's the dictionary on the line
The felon that took your mind.
It took it... and mixed it with bacon.
It's good. It's fat, but it was taken.

Chewed. Digested. Ready to expel it out.
Did you hear it this time?
From the wire-line zapped to your mind.
Now that you hear it... here's your spine.

Flip, flip, flip
Flip the dictionary
A red canary
What do you wanna bury?

# Liberty and Death

No need to ask
For liberty or for death
You are born with both
They are both your gift

No matter the pace
You run your race
You have the liberty
To guide or chase

They can't make you eat
They can't make you sleep
They cannot make you move
Or speak.

Don't feel. Don't hear.
Don't see. Don't fear.
You cannot control everything
But you have liberty
To control your fears.

Liberty is the death
Death is the liberty
By any means necessary
Give me death or give me liberty.

# To Swallow Pain

To swallow pain
Down a narrow throat
The tears of sorrow
The only hope.

# You Can't Fake It

When you bake it
You can't fake it
Just take it
Go
See if you make it

You're in the race
But you're moonwalking
Backwards
Just moon-talking

I'm tip-topping
Too high to understand
You under-stand me
Buried deep
Swimming in the bottom
Of the sea

The heat
The pressure
You get it?
It's depth

You can't afford the tools
To see deeper
A trade-off too large
A titanic to an ocean's bay

Don't play with me
Don't pass my way
I throw spinning kicks
I'll snap your leg

# **Get Those Carrots**

Pull them carrots
Chop them thin
Dry them out
With the wind

Two carrots
Turn to stones
Hold them tight
Take them home

You know that men
Will kill for food
The two carat stones
They'll take that too

Shadow your carats
Within the dark
The light will show
A sensual spark

To risk it all
For works of dirt
A shameful swim
In the lake called hurt

It has been told
Leave your desires
On the boat
At the shore

When you touch
The new land
Leave your stones
In the sand

# I Hate. I Hate. I Hate.

I hate
When I can not
Get it

I hate
When I'm not
With it

I hate
How I'm
Passed by

I hate
When death
Comes by

I hate
When I
Lose sight

I hate
When I
Don't fight

I hate
When the
Day ends

I guess I just hate
When the
Day begins

# Hunger of the Wise

I no longer
Seem to wonder
Of that hunger
Of the wise

A man will fool you
Drowning you with disguise.

There is nothing like
The pain of the wise
The scabs of their lessons
Never seem to subside

# An Endless Dome

The paws of kittens
Now does the killings
Snout red as Rudolph's
Sharp claws in mittens.

I was that cat
Who wished to be
A jungle King
A sage with things

I had something same
But it went lame
No drips.
No drops.
No shower of fame.

But within my light
I take the flight
Overnight
To the fight

To the battle
I carry stones
No words to say
An endless dome

# Take a Man's Home

Stone by stone
I break the dome
Here I stand
In your home

I got the spoon
The fork
The cup

It's time to eat
I'll eat your luck

I take the cup
And pour some punch
Blood flavor
The rest is yuck!

I don't dodge
Or dip
Or duck

I took your lodge
You
You suck

I take your house
And your spouse

I take your gold
The rest is sold.

# My Mistake

My mistake
I had to swerve
I had to brake
I had to turn

You see that urn?
He didn't turn
He had a chance
But now he's burned

The lesson here
The lesson learned
A flash of life
It's time to turn

Up a hill
My mistake
Down a cliff
Into the lake

Trust your gut
And trust your mind
They will grant you
More life and time.

I should have learned
When to turn
Case closed
My mistake

# The Scene Seen

You tell me
What I see
But what I see
Is nothing to me

The fee you seek
Earned week to week
I'd need a tweak
To reach that peak

You talk and talk
But globs I hear
That's why I walk
Right past here

Don't you worry
I heard you clear
I just don't carry
What you dear

Stop your foot steps
Don't you follow
Your creepy foot steps
Sound so hollow

I've told you once
I'll say this twice
I'd have to work months
To afford that price

But what I see
Is nothing to me
So, you tell me
What I see.

# Stay True

Within the Tiger's Eye
Is where I lie
And in my eye
Is where you die

You see
It's a sight
Your eye
It shows fright

My inside tuition
It is price-less
Call it... In-tuition
It is Ice-Less

Yours is lifeless
Where the knife is
You're in a crisis

You should see this
This is priceless
My eyesight is

You have funny glasses
Thick as icebergs
Stuck with the masses.

# **Down the Hill**

Oh Boy
Here we go
Down the hill
On the go

By the toad
On the rock
Loop around
Birds that talk

Still on pace
In this race
Bump by bump
Case by case

Swift through vines
Plucking thorns
Almost there
Sound the horns

My strong will
Is my wheel
So, roll with me
Down the hill

# The
# END...

# About the Author

Born, in 1983, to an African American family (descendent from slavery) in Salinas, California, Lawrence Murphy Jr. joined the United States Army at age eighteen to become a United States Army Airborne Ranger. During his service, he deployed four times to combat zones: two times in support of Operation Enduring Freedom (the war in Afghanistan, 2001) and two times in support of Operation Iraqi Freedom (the war in Iraq, 2003). After his military service, Lawrence Murphy Jr. pursued studies of business finance at Fresno State University, achieving distinction; earning the graduating status of cum laude. During college, he met his wife. They have two children. Lawrence enjoys reading, writing, studying martial arts, watching movies, and enjoys warm spring afternoons with family and friends.

Follow the author on **social media**:

- Instagram      @lq.murphy
- TikTok      @lqmurphy
- Twitter      @LQ_murphy
- LinkedIn      linkedin.com/in/lawrencemurphyjr

# "Gift Yourself Insightful, Therapeutic Poetry"

- ## *The I in my Eye*
  *L.Q. Murphy*

  Dark poetry with art ready to help you rethink the world. Intense emotions from the poetry make the mind rethink. Poetry and art help readers learn more about human nature. This book is a mixture of poetic themes. **eBook, paperback, and hardcover (on Amazon.com)**

- ## *Broken Scabs*
  *L.Q. Murphy*

  Offered to you is the immense emotional poetry about the sharp pains of life, similar to a broken scab. Like the scab, we use poetry to heal and become better people. The book contains five themes of life. Each theme section contains poetry written to remedy emotional wounds. Scabs. They can be to either our pity or they can be the opportunity to learn and improve. **eBook, paperback, and hardcover (on Amazon.com)**

# <u>Afterword</u>

# "Thank YOU"